THE SPIRIT WORLD

Where Love Reigns Supreme

PHILIP BURLEY

Also from Mastery Press:

Mastery
Press

Love Knows No End

Heart's Healing

The Blue Island
Beyond Titanic – Voyage into Spirit

The Hum of Heaven

The Wisdom of Saint Germain

The Gift of Mediumship

Awaken the Sleeping Giant

A Legacy of Love
Volume One: The Return to Mount Shasta and Beyond

To Master Self is to Master Life

A Wanderer in the Spirit Lands

THE SPIRIT WORLD

Where Love Reigns Supreme

PHILIP BURLEY

Mastery
Press

Phoenix, Arizona

Dedication

To all of those in the heavenly spheres
who have served each of us on earth with
unselfish, unfailing love and devotion.

Acknowledgments

Every book is the result of numbers of people working individually and together to bring it into existence, and *The Spirit World, Where Love Reigns Supreme* is no exception. You know who you are, and you have my unending gratitude. However, because of the nature of this writing, I want to forego the usual recognition of those on earth who helped make this book possible and acknowledge exclusively all those working with me from the other side of life as they have done over the years. Your dedicated and consistent interfacing with my small efforts gave rise to a lifetime of exposure to the spirit world and closely related topics. The results of your ongoing guidance and support are apparent in this book, as well as in others I have written.

I thank and acknowledge each one of you, known and unknown, for your presence in my life, the abundant love, wisdom, and spiritual insight you have given me, and the inspiration and urging that leads me to share it with others.

Contents

Preface

Life after death or life in a dimension beyond earth, sometimes called *the spirit world*, is a subject of hope for many, doubt for some, and fear for others. There are also those who believe in life after death because they have read about it and simply have faith that it exists. For me, life after death is the logical outcome of a life lived in this limited dimension called earth. Death of the physical body is not a choice. It happens to everyone. What is the purpose of life and death? And what happens when we die?

We all recognize that life is essentially about love—love of self and others. The nature of true love is such that we do not want it to end. This is why we grieve when someone we love dies. We feel sorrow because we have lost the object of our love, a love that we could exchange only with that special person, mate, child, parent, or friend. In addition to the fact that we do not want to cease to exist, our need to love and be loved is why we hope and pray for life beyond this life. We long to rejoin those we have loved and continue to experience the peace and joy intrinsic to love. If you have truly loved someone who has died, you know exactly what I mean. Grief is a universal experience that comes from missing someone who is no longer in the physical world. We miss the exchange of mutual love that we had before the death of our loved one.

The enduring nature of our desire to love and be loved can only come from a creator whose essential nature is love—eternal, unconditional love. The need and desire to forgive also comes from this nature of love that is stronger than any negative emotion. Such love seeks a way to restore former love or love betrayed. Out of this love is born the need to forgive and the act of forgiving. Love and forgiveness are two sides of the same coin.

Without a continuation of love beyond earth, the eternal quality of true love could not be manifested. Then what would be the point of having such love at all? It would be a cruel invention of the creator to give us the experience of love with someone and then take it away so that we could never again experience it with our loved one. This is why I see life after death as a logical outcome of life lived in this limited dimension of earth.

Beyond this logical deduction, there are some who know from direct experience that life does not end with physical death. Perhaps you are one of those people. I am. Since I was born with the gift of perceiving the spirit world, and was consciously aware of it at the tender age of four, I can say directly, boldly, and without hesitation that life goes on beyond physical death. Because of my experience, I have a burning desire to share what I know to take fear out of death for as many people as possible.

I work on many fronts to bring understanding to searching people everywhere regarding the question, "Is there life after death?" To this end, and with an eye toward even greater enlightenment than taking the sting of fear out of death, I have prepared this book, not only to confirm our survival of death, but to explain how we will live in the life beyond. This is not a long-winded treatise about life after death, but rather a touching on the necessary and obvious regarding the continuation of life. It is the simple story of how we, as eternal spiritual beings, will celebrate eternal life and eternal love, not only with all whom we have loved on earth, but with the Creator and all enlightened citizens of those holy spheres of love and light.

The content of *The Spirit World, Where Love Reigns Supreme* is derived primarily from my own life experience, combined with what others have told me, and what I have gleaned from extensive research. I have also learned much through giving thousands of spiritual readings during my twenty-two-year career of work as a spiritual sensitive or medium.

Because of my first-hand experience, I understand the ramifications of knowing or not knowing about the spirit world, so I urge everyone to get as much understanding as possible about it. One day, without fail, you will find yourself in that world which is the destiny and destination of all. You will be there, not by merit, but by the divine right of passage called death. Only it is *not* death, after all. It is the stepping out of your physical body, as an eternal spirit, born into a world without end that is beyond your present ability to comprehend. It is your birthright.

Thank you for this opportunity to come into your life to share what has been so readily and generously shared with me from my early childhood until now. My hope is that the contents of *The Spirit World, Where Love Reigns Supreme* will bring you new insight about the world ahead, so that you may be most prepared for your eventual existence in the spirit world. I have written it with you in mind.

— Philip Burley

Spirit World Reality

I am so familiar with the spirit world that I can simply tell it like it is, based on my long, consistent and various experiences with the other side. I do not have to stop and think about the spirit world because it is a part of the fabric of my life. Those who have grown up with a language don't have to stop and think about sentence construction before they speak. This is what seems to have happened to me during decades of studying the spirit world, living through countless spiritual experiences, and sharing what I have learned. I am greatly blessed because of this.

When William Peter Blatty's book, *The Exorcist*, came out in 1973, I gave a talk at the University of Colorado, in Boulder, on the extraordinary phenomena described in the book and explained what was actually taking place. Two hundred and fifty students who gathered had so many questions and generated such a lively discussion that no one wanted to go home! At that time, I was one of the few people involved in the study of spirit world, and it took courage to speak about my experience, because the general population was not well versed about the world of spirit, and many considered it as something weird. Fortunately, that's no longer the case.

People today are more interested in the reality of the spirit world than ever before. Some are curious, and others experience spiritual phenomena in prayer and meditation, or while going through the normal routines of life. There are numerous fiction and non-fiction stories of angels, out-of-body experiences, and spirit visitations, and books on the subject have been increasingly popular over the last two decades. There is a current spiritual awakening in America and throughout many parts of the world.

Understanding the reality of the spirit world is necessary if we are to live the best life we can live on earth. Once we know that how we live today will affect our lives in the spirit world, life takes on new meaning. Once we are sure God is real, love and life are eternal, and we will personally survive our deaths, we no longer fear dying. We may fear the process, or the difficulties we'll encounter on the way, but we anticipate the moment of death in a new light, because we know we will continue to live and love in another dimension.

Indeed, the "veil," as some call it, is getting thinner between the spiritual and physical worlds, and more and more people are aware that we exist simultaneously in both spheres. We are connected to earth through our physical senses and our physical body. We already live in "heaven" as spiritual beings with spiritual senses. We have lost much of our spiritual sensitivity because of discouraging cultural or even religious views, but all we have to do is go inside to listen, look, and feel, and we know we are already there.

Mediums, Mind Readers, and Mystics

Among those familiar with the concept of spirit world, the word *medium* means a person who literally serves as a bridge between this world and the spirit world by communicating with those on the other side through clairaudience, clairvoyance, clairsentience, or intuition, with or without the use of palm reading, physiognomy, tarot cards, tea leaves, or other tools.

Mind readers or psychics are sometimes mediums and sometimes not. They may be unaware of spirit communication and simply experience a knowingness about someone by focusing on that person. Whether they are aware of it or not, spirit world provides much of the information, directly or indirectly. Some talented mediums or psychics are famous, and others are unknown to most of the world. Some have natural gifts they choose not to use in a professional or disciplined way. With both mediums and psychics, there are all degrees of talent and development, just as there are among musicians and those in many other fields.

Throughout history, mystics have been people who have spiritual experiences with God, angels, and spirit beings from the highest realms. Many, like Joan of Arc, have seen visions or heard voices, so they, too, had gifts of clairvoyance and clairaudience. Some have experienced phenomena such as stigmata. Others have had special powers of healing. There have been extensive examples of prophecy, especially in the Old Testament books of the Bible, but also in modern times, through people such as Jeane Dixon or Edgar Cayce. For centuries, Eastern mystics have taught their disciples the art of meditation as a practice leading to inner wisdom and spiritual enlightenment. What all mystics have in common is a singular devotion to God or to the spiritual path.

I am a professional medium who was born with natural gifts, and I have had three years of formal training in my field. I have consistently practiced meditation and journaling for many years to develop my skills, and I have taught meditation and spiritual development to others. I give spiritual readings to people all over the world, and I'm usually booked fairly far in advance. For some time, I gave readings only in person, but I have found that using the telephone is also effective, and it provides more people with access to readings. The most consistent characteristic of my mediumship is my interest in how our spiritual experiences enhance our relationship with God. Some have said that I am a mystic more than a medium, because my relationship with God is the foundation of my life and the basis for all of my spiritual experiences.

I was raised a Lutheran and attended a Methodist church, but I have studied many religions and faiths. I had profound spiritual experiences from the time I was four years old and continue to have them now. As a child, I couldn't wait to go to bed, because night after night, I would rise out of my body and see, hear, and feel such wonderful spiritual energies. In my youth and in my adult life, I have had dreams and visions of Jesus, who has spoken with me about the work that I do, and I have received what I can only call an anointing from him. I've also had direct experiences with the heavenly Father, both in dreams and when awake.

I have been consulted by psychologists and psychiatrists about spirit influence as it occurs in spirit obsession or possession in mental hospitals. One psychiatrist in a group I spoke to said that he struggled with accepting the information in one of my talks. I looked at him across the table and said, "It's not my problem. Your lack of experience does not discourage me, because I *know* from experience that the spirit world exists." So, when I speak with conviction, it's not because I'm trying to convince anyone. It's because the spirit world *is*. It is more real than we are.

What Happens When We Die?

God created the physical world out of spiritual energy, and the ideal or blueprint for the physical world first existed in God's mind and in the spirit world. After the due process of planning the creation of the physical world, God brought it into existence. The physical world and the spiritual world are not separate worlds, but a continuum of reality. It is similar to this example: If you apply heat to ice, which is solid, it turns to water, evaporates, and becomes steam. Gradually, the steam becomes invisible to our eyes, but it's still water in a different form. The earth is like the ice—solid and visible to our physical eyes. The spirit world is like the steam as it becomes invisible.

The spirit world is part of the continuum of our experience. It is actually just as substantial as the physical world, and we will experience this when we can see, hear, touch, and feel it through our spiritual senses. Spirits are able to lower their vibration to interact with those in the physical world, and we in the physical world can raise our vibration, through meditation or attunement, to meet them halfway. The spiritual world is here with us now, and we are already spirits who *temporarily* have physical bodies that allow us to move freely within the physical world. The two worlds interpenetrate and pass through each other, but the spirit world vibrates at a higher frequency than our physical senses can discern. We already know that there are elements of energy, colors, and sounds that are beyond the spectrum of our physical senses. The spirit world is just as real; but it is imperceptible to us if we use only our physical senses.

If the lights in a room were completely turned out, then no matter how bright our clothing or other objects in the room were, we wouldn't be able to see them. That's because the eye is not what causes us to see. The light reflected from an object is what enables us to see it. This light goes through the eye to the brain, where it registers as information about the object we are viewing. What light is to the physical eye and physical brain, understanding is to the spiritual eye and spiritual mind. Without understanding the existence of the spirit world, you can't see it. At the time of your death, even if a spiritual being stood right in front of you, waving his arms to try to get your attention, you wouldn't see him, and your initial adjustment to living in the spirit world would be far more difficult. Spirit beings have told me that the energy of many in that world is spent trying to help people who die in such a state.

So far, I've met no one who can escape leaving the physical body at some point! Every day, hundreds and thousands of people die without even realizing what has happened. The tragedy of this is that people who know nothing about the spirit world can't experience its comfort and beauty when they pass over. In fact, such people are often confused to the point that they become lost and remain erroneously attached to the earth plane.

You may have read about people who have had out-of-body or near-death experiences. Many describe a glorious experience after going through the tunnel, where they see a brilliant light and meet loved ones who have died or religious figures who mean much to them. They write or speak of being in the presence of such beauty and love that they don't want to return to this world. It's less well known that a significant number of people close to death have experienced darkness or confusion and, more specifically, have encountered entities of the lower realms of spirit. When experiencing these darker dimensions, they feel fearful, confused, and lost. When they come back into their bodies, they talk about being very disturbed by these spiritual dimensions, and they definitely don't want to be there ever again. But that's where they *were*.

Because they have visited different areas of the spirit world, people near death have had both positive and negative experiences. This is an indication of what anyone might experience in the moments following physical death, and it demonstrates the importance of being prepared for entering the spirit world. It's why I've dedicated my life, not to spirit manifestation, but to bringing understanding regarding the existence and nature of the spirit world.

The biggest confrontation that we face after entering the spirit world is a review of our own lives. When we have this experience, we accurately judge ourselves, though people have varying capacities to understand their own lives and know what to do to correct past mistakes. The best way to be prepared is to review our lives while we are alive on earth and do what we can to change or make amends before passing into the spirit world.

Emmanuel Swedenborg was a wonderful mystic of the seventeenth century who wrote many volumes describing his spiritual experiences. He said that he went into the spiritual world while he was alive, where he met Jesus and many high spirits. While he was there, he observed a man who had been a wealthy and influential member of London society. When the man first arrived in the spirit world, his life, like a movie, passed in front of him. Swedenborg and other spirits could see what he was watching, but the man himself saw his life most clearly, and he was the one who experienced the full impact of the life review.

As Swedenborg watched, he observed a grave in front of the wealthy man. He saw another man crawl out of this grave who said, "You murdered me." The prominent man was horrified, because he had successfully covered up a murder he had committed in London. He had never told another person about it, and it had never been discovered. But in the spirit world, there are no secrets.

The most important thing that we experience through reviewing our lives is not seeing what we have done to someone else, but feeling how that person has felt as a result. We experience the feelings of those we have affected as we re-experience our lives. If someone became bitter because of what we did and abused other people because of that, then we see this chain reaction and feel its effects on that person's family and on other people. We also see and feel the extended results of all the good that we have done.

How everything weighs out determines where we go within the spirit world. This is a just and merciful result, because we are most comfortable where our true nature and vibration match exactly the place where we reside in spirit. Because this is true while we're still on earth, we are often drawn to people who think and feel as we do.

What happens if we die after a serious illness? If a person dies in a hospital bed, the physical body remains in the bed until it is taken away, but the spirit of the person will enter the spirit world, complete with a spiritual body. Depending on the spiritual awareness and condition of the person who has died, spirit beings may actually come with a stretcher beside the bed, pick up the person, and take him or her to the spiritual counterpart of a hospital in the spiritual world. It is more like a place of rest in the spirit world, where a person who has been ill can experience healing. Many people benefit from this experience before moving on.

When people pass into the spirit world, particularly if they've had a prolonged illness, have been in an accident, or died suddenly in their sleep, they may not understand what has happened to them. Do you recall being in a very deep sleep when someone wakes you up, and you feel disoriented? That's the way it is when we pass into the spirit world without realizing it. Sometimes people who die while they are sleeping stand up beside their physical bodies, get out of bed, and walk right through the bedroom door, even though it's not open. Their intention is just to go to the kitchen to get a drink of water, just as they have done every other morning. Suddenly they find out that everything has changed, but they don't understand what happened.

In an airplane crash where many people die, I'm sure that most of them are in a daze because they don't realize what has happened. Everything happens so fast that they can't be sure they survived. But people in the spirit world who know about the crash ahead of time are standing by to help them make the transition. Those who died in the accident will be taken to a place of rest where they can regain their mental and emotional equilibrium.

Stories told from the other side indicate that children go to a level of the spirit world that is very close to God because of their innocence. They don't have anything to undo, but they have missed the opportunity to grow through the struggles of this earthly life. As we live in this physical body, learn to crawl, walk, talk, and meet many other challenges, our physical brain and intellect grow. If it is known that an adult on earth has missed the crawling stage, and has resultant problems, he may be taken through patterns of crawling to gain what he did not gain as a child.

Children who die are taken care of immediately. They are safe from harm, since there is no destruction in the spirit world, so they don't have to be protected from physical danger as they are here on earth. They are usually cared for in small groups with a spiritual being who was a very loving parent on earth. They go to school, as they would on earth, though learning happens much more quickly in the spirit world. They continue to visit their families on earth and observe the life of their parents and siblings. They help and inspire their families and, in that way, continue to grow.

When we sleep at night, our spirits rise up out of our bodies, and we go into the spiritual world. When a child dies, either parent may wake up the next morning and say to the other, "I had the most beautiful dream. I saw Timmy and held him, and we talked. He was so real." That *is* a real experience. But as we move through the vortex of physical energy and re-enter the physical body, there is a change in vibration, and we are in a denser vibration. The memory of our experience begins to change because it belongs to the spiritual mind. It is still very clear in the spiritual mind, but we access it only as a vague memory or dream.

If people lose a mate at whatever time of life, they visit with their mates at least in dreams or in conversations in their minds. Their mates may materialize in a more substantial way, appearing before their spiritual sight or providing signs of their presence. They continue to observe and participate in each other's lives, and in this way, they're comforted. No matter what our age or situation at the time of death, all that happens to us and to our loved ones remaining on earth happens according to just spiritual law, based on divine love.

Ignorance of the spirit world reality is a source of many problems, because people fear what they don't understand. That's why it's important for people to understand as much as possible about the spirit world before passing into it. Read as many books as you can, but use judgment regarding what information to accept. If the material turns you off when you first read it, it is probably not for you, at least not at that time. If the information is positive and makes sense to you, it may be something you can adopt for yourself, at least as a working concept. While some of the material in books will not be meaningful to you, get whatever understanding you can. As you study, keep an open mind, so that you can continue to be guided to still higher truth.

Through giving readings, listening to people, studying books, and learning from my spiritual guides and teachers, I know how important it is for people to understand what will happen once we leave this body, and I'm determined to help as many people as possible to have at least a beginning understanding of the spirit world. Since I have a good working knowledge of it, I feel responsible to share that information. I often tell my students, "Once you know about the spirit world, try to help your relatives and friends understand, even if indirectly, by giving them books to read on the subject. Give them whatever information you think they're ready for, but try to educate them. It will make a difference to them when they enter the spirit world."

My purpose is not to sell anyone on the existence of the spirit world or to push some kind of ism, theology, or religion down anyone's throat. The spirit world is a universal reality whether people know it or not. Every person—Gentile, Jew, Catholic, Protestant, black, white, green, red, pink, or *whatever*, are all going to experience the spirit world at some point. Therefore, my job is to tell as many people as I can about it. They will respond as they choose, but I hope many will go back to their churches, synagogues, organizations, friends and family and share what they have learned.

Levels of the Spirit World

Within our own towns or cities, there are people who are very good and people at the other extreme. Anywhere we go, we find selfless people and selfish people. In this contemporary life and in history, we see all degrees of spiritual evolution, from saints who give up their lives for others, to people who commit acts of evil against their fellow human beings.

People who live in the spirit world also exist at all degrees of spiritual evolution, but there is an important difference: In our physical world, two people at different levels of spiritual development can be in the same room, such as the waiting room of a doctor's office. In that situation, we don't know another person's level of spirituality. We can't tell whether a person is loving or cruel, though we may have an instinctive response that gives us an indication. Unlike those gathered in the doctor's office on earth, beings in the spirit world gather with those who have reached a similar degree of spiritual growth.

Because people don't know about spiritual evolution, they're not aware that spirits at various levels may be very close to people on earth. Often, we are blessed by visits from those in the spirit world who are there to support, help, encourage, and guide us. We may be visited by angels who are pure spirit and have never taken a physical body, or by human beings who were loving and good when they lived on earth. Sometimes our relatives come close to help and inspire us. According to one dictionary, one definition of the word "inspiration" is *divine guidance or influence exerted directly on the mind and soul of humankind.* Who is doing this guiding and influencing? It is the Creator, and those in spirit who are working with us, including the angelic portion of the spirit world.

I have experienced conflicting testimonies about the spirit world, even from those who live there. For example, some say that we don't eat in the spirit world, and others say, yes, we do eat in the spirit world. Both can be true, depending on our level of spiritual development when we enter the spirit world. If we are close to the earth plane, in the astral area, then life there is very much like it is here. There are department stores, grocery stores, restaurants, cars, airplanes, and every amenity that we have here. But there is no money exchanged. We can just go into a store to get goods. People do eat in this realm. All of this happens because the mind is still working as though we are in the material world, so we essentially create a nearly identical world there.

Throughout the spirit world, from the lowest to the highest realms, the energy for life is derived from God's presence. This is a fact on earth as well, whether we know it or not. The ultimate truth is that God is the origin of all energy, all life. This energy, at the core, is the very love of God that penetrates and surrounds all of his creation. Scientists have yet to discover the origin of the atom and what enables it to exist and to function as it does everywhere. The basis for its creation, existence, operation, and maintenance is the invisible, immeasurable love of God.

Regardless of the degree to which one can receive this energy, all in the realms of light in the spiritual world readily acknowledge that the atmosphere they breathe and bask in is the presence of God. It is manifested through the great central sun that is always shining forth with God's love and truth, from which the inhabitants derive their very life.

Those in the highest realms partake of this reality to the greatest extent because they have greater understanding and experience in love, and this makes it possible for them to directly receive God's energy. Those in lesser realms lack full understanding and experience in love. It is as though clouds of ignorance and misunderstanding appear between the "sun" and the beings in these realms, blocking a more direct and ultimate experience of God.

Those in the higher realms realize that nourishment comes through understanding and love, and they know that the closer one is to God, the less energy is needed from any other source. Those in the very highest level of the spirit world are those who have experienced that God lives within them and they and God are one. They dwell in constant peace, joy, and love, which they call bliss, and have access to all knowledge. They are the masters of masters. Of all humanity, they live closest to God. Jesus is one of them.

Cities of the earth also exist on various levels in the spirit world. New York City, for example, exists in the spirit world in the highest to the lowest level. In the low realms, New York City has residents who have not evolved spiritually, and the city appears as it is in its worst light. In higher realms, we will find a New York City that is more refined, where there are good people who lived righteous lives. Their New York City has none of the lower elements in it, and all the best qualities of the city are there. Two people on earth can own identical furniture from the same store, but if their internal spirit lives and external behaviors are very different, the vibration of the objects in their homes will reflect this and be distinctly different, too.

For those in the higher realms of the spirit world, the number one reason for being is to serve. Jesus said that whoever is greatest among us is the servant of all. That is because people who serve in this way are emulating God. As God takes care of his children, his love pours out on all of us. Those who would be close to God would do well to serve others in the same way. That is the very nature of the higher beings in the spirit world. They have become love itself.

The highest levels of the spiritual world are filled with saints who emulated the loving and serving nature of God. They are people of all religions who lived for the sake of others. These individuals lived single-mindedly for God, sacrificing themselves in service for the love of God and humanity. Because of the way they lived their lives, they raised their spirits to a very high level on earth and in the spiritual world.

Those who live in the brightest light of the spirit world, as opposed to those who live in ignorance or in the darker realms, know that the way to build true character and grow spiritually, is not acquiring for yourself, but helping others. They want as much for others as they want for themselves, or more. In this way, the spirit world is a hierarchy of love and loving service. The degree of our love for other people through service in this life will determine where we will live in the spiritual world when we pass over.

If you have been a person who has loved others sacrificially, as much or more than yourself, and sought to help them as much as you could, then you will be in a very high place in the spiritual world. If you have lived for yourself and your motives were always to get things for yourself and worry about yourself, your place in the spirit world will not be as high. Your motives will be the standard by which you are judged, and your place in the spirit world will be a direct reflection of the degree of your love. If you have a big heart, and you truly have loved others as much or more than yourself, then your home in the spirit world will not only be large, but also exquisitely beautiful.

In saying all of this, I do not mean that it is wrong to love yourself. If you don't, who will? Only if we love ourselves will we take proper care of ourselves, and it is on this basis that we can properly love and care for others. Love for self and love for others are not mutually exclusive loves. It is a matter of our keeping our priorities straight and finding a balance between these two loves.

I have a friend who lives like a saint. He told me about a dream where he was taken into the spirit world and shown around by a spirit guide. The guide said, "I want to take you to your home." My friend said, "Philip, I could not believe how beautiful it was. I kept saying to the guide, 'I am just not worthy. I'm not worthy of this.' But the guide said, 'You built it. You built it with your unselfish love.'" My friend described the home the guide showed him. He said there were big rooms, with furniture covered with gold or jewels. He said, "I didn't think I could ever create a place like that." In the dream, my friend told his guide, "I don't want to go back. I want to stay here. It's just so beautiful." He didn't want to leave until he started thinking about his wife and children on earth and found himself being drawn back to his physical body. When he woke up, he was lying in his bed.

People who live in the spirit world have given many testimonies about how the true dimension of our love affects what we can expect to find when we arrive on the other side. As we live on earth, we are actually building the place we will occupy in the spirit world. The vegetable, animal, and mineral kingdoms and everything in the area where we are will be a direct and accurate reflection of the state of our lives on earth. Plants and flowers reflect the degree of our understanding, animals reflect the degree of our love, and minerals reflect our will.

The highest realms have the most beautiful flowers that anyone could ever see, and the animals in those realms reflect great love. The homes are built of the largest and most exquisite gems.

Is There a Hell?

"Hell" is a name given to the lower realms of the spirit world, and these realms reflect a lack of love and understanding. There isn't much light, because light in the spirit world is generated by love and understanding. People who were poor in loving others, who lived for themselves, or abused, used, or ignored others may live in a little hovel. Even if they live in a larger home, the vibration of it will reflect the darker realm in which they live. There are less appealing forms of animal and plant life, representing the lower attributes of the human spirit. Spirit beings who dwell in these realms may even appear distorted or less than human if they lived more like animals while alive on earth.

In our earthly society, prison environments reflect the lower realms of the spirit world. The spiritual energy in prisons is often lower than in many other places, and we can feel this if we walk through areas housing inmates who have committed the worst crimes. People are incarcerated to pay for crimes committed, but there are often no effective programs for their redemption. Inmates then become even more cynical and bitter during their stay in prison, because of the way they are treated by prison staff and each other, and they return to committing crimes when they are released. According to Wikipedia in the year 2003, in the United States, sixty-eight percent of males and fifty-eight percent of females are rearrested. Fifty-three percent and thirty-nine percent, respectively, are re-incarcerated.

Not all spirits who visit us are from the higher realms of the spirit world, and there are instances when spirits can affect people in adverse ways, particularly causing mental or emotional distress or confusion. Spirit beings who gather in prisons include those who have been executed and those who have died during long sentences. They have not found their way to a better spiritual reality after death, so they stay near individuals currently in prison, participating in their depression and bitterness. They even intensify negative emotions and foment unrest and criminal behavior within the prison walls. One of the reasons that a high percentage of people who leave prison end up incarcerated again is spirit influence, especially where crimes committed have involved alcohol and drug abuse, rape, or murder.

A number of people in prison were abused as children in various ways, including sexually, and so were victims themselves. They have a built-in sense of failure from the beginning of their lives, and they have a long-standing basis for lower spirits to bother them. Each of us has an energy field around us called an aura. When someone is very young, the aura is very open, so when a young child is abused, the child becomes a victim of low self-esteem and negative spirit influence at the same time. From study and personal stories, I know that some people are so influenced by low spirits that they commit crimes in a trance-like state and don't even know what they have done until after it has happened.

There was a story in the news several years ago about a woman who was traveling across the

United States with her Marine husband. All of their kitchenware was in the car, and as they were traveling through Oklahoma, the woman pulled a butcher knife out of the back seat and stabbed her husband repeatedly. Afterward, she didn't know she had done it. It is easy to conclude, "Oh, sure, she'll say anything," but lower spirits who are confused, angry, and bitter can invade people and take over to such a degree that the individuals will be literally "beside themselves," and not in control of their behavior. Many crimes of passion are committed because of these low level spirit influences.

People in prison need to have information about spirit influence so that they can be more assertive in stepping out of the spiritual atmosphere that may otherwise overwhelm them. They could have an awakening that could help them to find themselves. I have corresponded with several people in prison, and when I explained the spirit world and spirit influence, they gained a new understanding of their experience, realizing that their circumstances are not entirely because of them. The important thing to remember is that such individuals are still part of the human family. They are our brothers and sisters, and it would be good to maintain compassion for them, even as we protect ourselves and society from their actions.

We tend to make God in our image. We make God a lawgiver rather than a lover of humanity. Because God has the nature of a parent, he loves us as his children. This means that he must have the innate desire to have people with him. Many believe that some people are bound for eternal heaven and some for eternal hell. I would like to ask them, "Do you think the God of love can be happy when some of his children are with him and some of them are separated from him? Could any parent be happy in that situation, especially when those children are suffering?" I think God must have a way to be able to bring people home through love, but still within the structure of divine law. Everyone must earn a way up, and there really is no free lunch. God's love must be applied within the proper structure to be love. There must be discrimination in love. People who let their love go in all kinds of directions are just *feeling*. True love is feeling directed correctly, and it all happens according to divine law. It may take some people several centuries to progress from where they are, because they have been so blinded by their belief system, or because of how they have lived, but I believe it will happen.

In mental health settings, some patients have been influenced by confused spirits to the point of spirit obsession or possession, but they may be treated without anyone discovering how this is contributing to their illness. Since psychiatrists are medical doctors, they look at patients from a physiological standpoint first and then from a psychological point of view. They prescribe various medicines, like other doctors do, to affect the brain or body chemistry of their patients and help people find their mental and emotional balance. However, they are not always able to heal people. I asked a group of psychologists and psychiatrists that I spoke to, "Would you not agree that the best that you are sometimes able to do is to help people cope, but not really heal them completely?" They all agreed.

This is one reason that groups of psychiatrists and psychologists have come to hear talks about the spirit world. They have treated people diagnosed, for example, with multiple personality disorder. In these instances, three or more personalities were expressing themselves through one person. They came to me to try to understand how the spirit world might be affecting their patients. It is true that the brains of people with schizophrenia or other kinds of mental illnesses may appear different when studied, and factors affecting each person may vary, but spirit influence can play a strong role.

Because of our ignorance about the spirit world and spirit influence, it is harder and more complicated to help people with mental or emotional problems, including those who act out in ways detrimental to others or to themselves. Those trying to help such people, whether they are professionals or family members, can't deal directly with a spirit who may be negatively influencing a person, because we don't know the spirit is there. Many can't even comprehend such an idea.

Without knowledge of spiritual laws, people aren't able to help themselves as they otherwise might. They allow their thoughts and behaviors to go in a direction that actually attracts less evolved spirits whose influence causes them further problems. When this influence is very strong, people sometimes do things that they themselves abhor. Then they may say, "I don't know what came over me," or "Something got into me." Spirit beings who were addicted to alcohol in life often hang out at bars where they attach themselves to those who are drinking. Spirit obsession frequently causes alcoholism or makes it harder to overcome. Spirits may overshadow someone and literally drive that person to drink, so that the spirit can again taste the flavor of alcohol and feel its effects. It is the same with excessive smoking or any excessive behavior. Spirit influence is likely to be either the primary cause or a complicating factor that makes it harder for a person to change.

The books included in the Bible were selected from a number of sources, and there were several versions of the creation story in Genesis, the first book of the Bible. According to a version of Genesis not selected, Adam and Eve were spiritually open before they fell from grace. The two had spiritual sight that allowed them to see the angelic world, and they could communicate directly with God. After the fall, they lost that power. This version of the story is in the Vatican library and has been published in the combining of the two books into one called *The Lost Books of the Bible and the Forgotten Books of Eden* (A & B Book Dist. Inc.,

March 1994, ISBN 1-881316-63-7). If this version of the Adam and Eve creation story had been included in the Bible, instead of the version that was chosen, we would have had a very different religious basis for our worldview in the Judeo-Christian traditions. Because it wasn't, people not only lack an awareness about their innate spiritual gifts but also about the nature of life after death, and they are often actively discouraged from learning about any of this reality by their spiritual teachers.

Spirit Guides and Teachers

I have written at some length about spirits who may cause problems in our lives, and it is important to understand this so that we can think and act in ways that do not attract spirits who will only intensify our struggles. But it is equally important to understand that we are surrounded by beings of light who lift us up, inspire us to accomplish things, encourage us to love others, and comfort us in times of sorrow. They do *not* run our lives, though they work very cooperatively with us. They will not break spiritual laws that are there for our good, and they would never want to do so. Less evolved spirits break laws in their own self-interest and encroach on our lives, causing spirit obsession and possession, but most of the spirits surrounding us are there to help, motivated by love. It is because of love for us and the desire for us to grow in merit that higher spirits will not do our work for us. They will not take over our minds and bodies and do everything through us, but they will inspire us and even give us specific suggestions to help.

Having raised three children, I can say that if it wasn't for the existence of angels and the human spirit world, most children would die before they were three years old. If we weren't watched over at the most vulnerable stage of our lives, we wouldn't make it. Parents can't watch each movement of their children around the clock, and spiritual protection is an important element of our survival when we are very young.

There are many dramatic stories of faith in times of sorrow. Sometimes we are deeply moved by loving beings from the spirit world who come close to comfort us. When we are very lonely, they encourage us. Understanding this, we can draw closer to God and the spirit world in times when we need this contact the most, allowing ourselves to be open to healing love. Spirit beings are with us twenty-four hours a day. This doesn't mean that each spirit who works with us or visits us is always there, but spiritual beings are in constant contact with the earth plane, and if there is a small or large need to help an individual, they will be there.

Those in our circle of spiritual guides and teachers help us with ordinary day-to-day life. Sometimes when we are simply driving down the road, we get an impression or even hear an urgent voice in our minds telling us, "Be careful around the next curve; there's an accident," or, "Slow down." Sometimes we may be warned about a bridge being washed out or get a flash of intuition that there is a problem with our bank account or the wiring in our homes. We may feel a strong inclination to have our health checked or our cars serviced. Spirit beings will remind us to call a certain person, or whisper in our ear that someone far away needs contact or encouragement. They may impress us to write a letter. I have had these kinds of experiences.

We usually receive such messages from spiritual beings who have taken on the assignment to help people on earth by inspiring and protecting them. Each person on earth usually has more than one guide, master teacher, friend, or relative who has accepted the mission of helping him or her throughout life.

Spirit guides and teachers often work with people in relation to their mission or occupation, and the group of spirits guiding you at the workplace may not be the same as those with you at home. Spirits with medical expertise or the ability to inspire a person to serve others may surround a nurse. A schoolteacher working with young students may be helped by a spirit being who was a good psychologist, teacher, or parent on earth. A homemaker will have someone, perhaps from her ancestry, who is able to help with raising children, managing the home, or resolving relationship issues.

At this moment, my spirit guides are showing me a picture where the attorney who stands in the courtroom and delivers his arguments before the judge and the jury has someone with him who was a very good trial lawyer, someone who teaches him, inspires him, works with him, and gives him ideas. This kind of thing happens with each one of us.

Why do spirits serve, help, inspire, encourage, and love us in this way? Their motivations are consistent with spiritual law: They are able to grow as they help us to grow, they can express their desire to love and serve, and they can apply their specific ability to help us fulfill our purpose or mission in life.

Sometimes, when we are in our fifties, sixties, and seventies, we see that our bodies are older, but our spirits and minds haven't matured as we might have wished. If we arrive in the spirit world not yet spiritually mature, it may be because we didn't spend enough time living for others. When we see in the spirit world the importance of spiritual growth, we work to help those on earth with their growth and continue to grow through this experience. No one in the spirit world condemns us if we haven't reached spiritual maturity, because the same is true for most people entering the spirit world, usually because we haven't understood spiritual law.

Everything, as they say, is relative, so it's also a matter of degree. Some who have not loved others very much quickly see the need and opportunity to grow by serving those still alive on earth. Some who have served others want to grow still further in love, so they too return. Spiritual masters who reside at the highest levels of the spirit world may have no personal need to serve those on earth in order to grow, but they do because it is a significant way to represent God—and to express the love they have become.

Some spirit beings work with relatives—those they loved in life, for whom they feel great compassion. For example, a husband in the spirit world may realize that his beloved wife misses him. Because he knows what she is going through, he will visit and comfort her. As she experiences the healing and comfort of his presence, he also benefits. In other cases, spirits return because they are elevated enough to become a guide or teacher for someone they may not have known on earth. They are drawn to work with someone who has a mission or interest similar to theirs, such as another artist, scientist, or teacher.

Spiritual guides and teachers are with us from the time we are born. They are assigned to us, or drawn to us, because of our missions in life. They will not be with us unless they have things in common with us. In other words, Einstein would probably not have a baseball player working with him! The bigger our mission on earth, the more spirits we have around us, working to help orchestrate the things that we are doing. The number and kind of spiritual beings around us always correlates to the size and scope of our mission.

At least two guardian angels are also assigned to us at birth. Angels are different from human spirits in that they have never had a physical body. They look like human beings but their vibration is different because they have not lived an earthly life, and their purpose is to serve mankind as representatives of the Creator. What is singularly noticeable about them is the love that pours from them. There is no adequate way to describe it. They love others sacrificially, much more than they love themselves. Their greatest desire is to love and help us, and it is their highest joy. That is the essence of what an angel is. They also serve as God's messengers, and they exhibit the kind of love God has for us. I can speak so specifically to this point because I have met my angels while wide awake and conversed with them directly and easily. I can never forget this most amazing and wonderful experience.

A question that people always ask me is this, "Who are my guides and teachers?" They want me to zero in and say, "Well, your guides are so and so." I do give that information in a private reading, but not in a public meeting unless its sole purpose is to give spiritual readings to individuals in the audience. In general, you can determine who is with you by asking one question: What do I love most in life? That will tell you who you are, because what you love is what you are. Jesus loved all humanity, so his ruling love was cosmic love. God loves everyone, and Jesus loved as God loved. That is why God was with Jesus. If you are an individual who loves your family, then you'll have someone with you who also loved their family. The greater your love, the greater the love is of the person who is with you.

The most important thing to remember in thinking about all of this is that we are responsible for our choices, not the higher or lower spirits around us. Higher beings will not control our actions or thoughts in ways that detract from our spiritual growth and development, and we are the only ones who can say no to lower beings who encourage us to act in ways that have a negative effect on us or others.

The Spirit Body

When a sponge is filled with water, it's hard to tell where the sponge ends and the water begins, because they interpenetrate each other. In the same way, the spirit world and the physical world interpenetrate each other. As a spiritual being, I have a physical body and a spiritual body that also interpenetrate one another. As I hold up an arm, there is a spiritual arm in close proximity.

Many years ago, when I was first getting into this work, I was in bed one night, trying to sleep, when it got very cold in the house. I got up, walked over to the thermostat on the wall, and stood on a register on the floor right beneath it. I was half asleep and half awake as I stood on the register and said to myself, "Well, because it's so cold, I'll turn up the heat." When I saw my arm go up to adjust the setting on the thermostat, it was shining so bright that it lit up the room! It was an arm of light! My physical arm continued to hang down by my side, but I was too tired to realize that I hadn't physically touched the thermostat, so I just went back to bed. Needless to say, it didn't get any warmer. I didn't put it all together to figure out what had happened until the next morning.

Around this time, I was teaching a lecture on the spirit world in Lawton, Oklahoma, when I saw a young man sitting in the front row of the audience. As he sat there, his eyes got huge as he looked at me. I suspected that he was seeing something that was blowing his mind, so I asked him, "What's wrong?" He said, "You have two heads!" Everyone laughed, as if this guy was drunk or something, but he wasn't. I said, "Tell me what you mean," and he said, "Well, you're looking at us with your head turned straight ahead, but I can see another head that's light. I mean, it's made of light. And it's looking over there in another direction."

Sometimes a teacher is talking to the class, and he looks off into the distance. You assume he is just thinking about what he wants to say, and soon he turns back to the class and begins talking again. Actually, the teacher's spiritual mind and spiritual perception may be trying to pick up some information from someone in the spirit world. It is almost as though he is scanning the spiritual realms for information, but he doesn't even know it.

When people have a leg or an arm amputated, they retain what is called a phantom limb, and they may feel itching or pain in the limb, even though it's not there anymore. Some have been known to get out of bed, forgetting they no longer have one of their legs. They will step out on the phantom limb, because their will is so centered on having a leg, and the reality is so strong that it solidifies enough for them to walk a few steps. After two or three steps, they fall down when they realize that the leg is not there.

Human beings are the intersecting point of the spiritual and physical worlds, or the bridge between the two worlds. God, who is spirit, makes his entrance into the physical world through us. We are designed to function as the center of these two worlds, perceiving the spirit world through the spiritual senses and the spiritual mind and perceiving the physical world through the physical senses and the brain.

I have been asked whether we need a physical body in the spirit world, like unto our physical body on earth. The answer is yes, but of a higher and finer vibration, and it is made of light. At the highest level, both bodies are for manifesting love. In other words, if you feel love in your heart and mind but have no means to outwardly express it, then how can you show that love? We manifest our love through the hands, through the feet for example as we walk toward someone on our wedding day, or through the whole body in marriage; and we use the body in many other ways to express love.

We remain finite in the spirit world for this purpose—the manifestation of love. Those most spiritually evolved, on earth and in the spirit world, are able to touch in with the Infinite and obtain the same expanded, invisible qualities, but they can return to their spirit world finite form as love dictates.

What I sometimes ask people is this: Why would a God of love create a world that is so different from the spirit world that when you get there, you won't even recognize it? What means most to you in life? Most people say that personal relationships are most important, including family, friends, and teachers. Creation itself, with its animals, plants, and the beauty of nature are also important. Whenever we can, we want to spend our time with people and things we love. When we go on vacation, we revive ourselves by going to beautiful places. We love to be outside because it is an expression of the Creator, whether we think of it that way or not. It also reflects aspects of us. You recognize the beauty in a flower because that beauty is also in you.

That's why the spirit world appears to be similar to earth in many ways. The beauty of earth, if you recall, originally existed in the spirit world. Things that exist there are even more intensely beautiful because they are rarified in terms of vibration or frequency, and we see, hear, touch, smell, and feel everything there with our more sensitive spiritual senses. Fruits and flowers in the highest levels of the spirit world are more exquisitely beautiful and delicate than any we have on earth. While earlier I stated that eating took place only in the lesser realms, there is eating in the highest realms too, if desired, so as to partake of the invigorating spiritual elements in fruit, for example, that cannot be had in the realms existing nearer the earth plane where everything is closer to the earthly vibration.

Much depends on the state of mind with which we enter the spirit world. Some people who are crippled on earth don't have an objective under-standing of the spiritual world, and their spiritual body will remain crippled until they realize that they don't have to be that way anymore. Once they understand this, everything changes, and they are well. If people die at an older age, they will appear old at first because that's how they are used to seeing themselves. When they realize that age is truly a state of mind, they appear as they did at the prime of life, usually between twenty-five and thirty years of age.

Our perception influences reality so much in the spirit world because what is in the mind is in objective reality there. There is no incongru-ence between our minds and our bodies. That is one reason that spiritual growth on earth is so important. A physically beautiful person on earth who is selfish on the inside may have recognizable features in the spirit world, but he or she will not appear to be beautiful. A physically ugly person who is kind and thoughtful on earth will appear very beautiful in the spirit world. Even in this life, we recognize this kind of spiritual beauty through the energy and vibration around such people, so in our hearts, we already know this.

My father passed over at the age of eighty-one and I have seen him clairvoyantly many times. He usually appears as a young man, and he has the energy and vibrancy of a young person. I recognize him immediately because of his vibration, which is undeniable because it reflects the essence of who he is.

I have met Jesus innumerable times: in dreams and at my bedside, usually in the early morning hours, and during spiritual readings for my clients. I have seen him with both my spiritual eyes and my physical eyes. Jesus has the youthful appearance of being in his mid-twenties, but when I had a chance to see him up close and look into his most magnificent, crystal clear blue eyes, it was like looking into eternity. In them, one can see the depth and wisdom of two thousand years. His eyes shone with age-old wisdom.

How Do Our Spiritual Senses Open?

D o you want to know how to develop your spiritual senses so that you can see, hear, or sense the spiritual beings who are present around you? This is an important question, and one to be answered with care. Opening the spiritual senses is not the first priority. According to spiritual law, our spiritual senses open as the *result* of right living. As we grow spiritually, our spiritual senses open naturally.

If we care about people, worry about people, call them up, and pray for them, there is a likelihood that we will either have dreams of them or get impressions from the spirit world when it is important to reach out to them. Parents who love their children often dream of them or have a sense about their welfare. This is because of the love element, the loving aspect within their nature. As this element develops within us, our spiritual senses will open, especially if we are aware of the reality of spirit world and welcome this development. As your love grows, your spiritual senses become more acute.

Keep in mind that some people who do not exhibit loving qualities may appear to have spiritual insights, and they can even make strong pronouncements, including predictions or warnings about your life or world events. This can actually be the result of the strong influence of lower spirits, and it usually is not difficult to make this distinction. Truth is accompanied by the vibration of love and the uplifting quality of wisdom. Trust your own heart and your own instincts to guide you.

When St. Francis first began his work, his spiritual senses were not open, but before he passed on, they were highly developed. Clare, one of his earliest disciples, had been a young woman of the world until she became his follower. Before she died, she was so ill that she couldn't go to Christmas Mass to celebrate the birth of Jesus. When the sisters of her order returned from the service, she told them that she hadn't missed the celebration after all. She related that as she lay on her bed, she heard the music in the chapel, and wanted very much to be there. All of a sudden, spirits came, picked her up, and lifted her from her bed. They carried her to the chapel where she could be present at the entire Mass. This spiritual experience happened to Clare not because she sought spiritual experiences, but because she loved sacrificially. She devoted herself totally to following St. Francis and the dictates of the order that she founded, the Order of Poor Ladies.

All people have spiritual sensitivities to a degree. We can feel or know certain things instinctively, and they are undeniable. It's like practicing any art; if someone has an inclination toward music, for example, the more that person practices, the better he or she will be at playing the piano and refining the art. Some people are born to be virtuosos at the piano, and others will never become virtuosos, even if they practice all their lives. They may play the piano well, but without the obvious gift that some are born with. In the same way, there are varying degrees to which people can perceive the spirit world. Some people have intuition and they may have accurate impressions about things without seeing something clairvoyantly. Others may totally deny spirituality because they have embraced a teaching or even a habit of thought that blocks their sensitivity.

Communication happens through the whole body and the whole spirit. In the spirit world, unencumbered by our earthly body, we are ten times more sensitive than on earth. Every cell of our spiritual body communicates, experiences, and feels things. The entirety of our spirit serves as the sensing mechanism of our being. If our spiritual senses are attuned and we meet someone, we instinctively know many things about the person. Because of the natural sensitivity of most human beings, appearances don't fool us for long. In the spirit world, when two people meet, they don't have to use words to communicate unless they want to. Each can feel what the other is thinking and sense each other's emotion. If a spirit being starts to go toward someone in the distance, it may become apparent that this person wants to be alone. If that happens, the one starting toward the other will comply. It's so much easier to communicate, because there is no guesswork!

One big reason that we are less sensitive in this life than we could be is that our focus is often on external things. Instead of having the goal to master our spirituality, we often focus on mastering materiality. There is nothing wrong with having and enjoying material things. It's why they exist. But our priorities are sometimes wrong. When I suggest that it's important to make spiritual growth a higher priority, I'm not speaking about external practices such as attending religious services. I'm talking about the way that one cares about people. That is how we experience genuine spiritual growth, not by dressing well, looking good, or even reading religious books and praying. Our levels of growth and love are reflected by how we treat others.

In Russia, there was a study using rabbits. I don't like the way they conducted the experiment, but I'm sharing it because it is revealing. Scientists took a mother rabbit thirty miles out to sea on a ship, leaving her litter on land. They had a telephone hookup between the ship and the laboratory so they could communicate during the experiment. While they were connected, they systematically killed each one of the baby bunnies. Every time they did this, the mother rabbit flinched, even though she was far away from where it was happening. If rabbits are that sensitive, how much more sensitive are human beings?

I feel very blessed to have been born with a certain level of natural ability to discern spirits, and I have been consciously aware of seeing them since I was four years old; but I'm still working on the opening and refinement of my spiritual senses. That's because my love is still growing. My ability to love and to sacrifice for others is still a work in progress.

In my work as a medium, I primarily use spiritual sight, hearing, and feeling, though sometimes I can smell spiritual fragrances. I give readings to people with my eyes closed, as I can see better that way! I can sometimes see clairvoyantly with my eyes open as well. Not long ago, as I did a reading for a man in California, I suddenly smelled smoke. With my eyes closed, I saw a house burning in front of me. I sensed the presence of someone from the spirit world connected to the scene before me, and said, "There is a woman here in spirit who had a house burn down, and who nearly died in the fire." He said, "Yes, my aunt. It's my aunt."

I said, "Well, she's here, and she comes more like a mother than an aunt, as she's standing in front of me and to my right." He said, "That's because my mother died when I was a child, and my aunt raised me." Because I was able to use my spiritual senses to perceive the reality of what had happened to his aunt as well as the nature of their relationship, he was able to accept that his aunt was really coming through.

When I have given readings for people associated in some way with Mohammed, he appears in a green and white striped turban, and I see him this way very clearly, even with my eyes closed. When this happens, I may be unaware that the person before me has a Muslim background, but I'll say, "Are you a Muslim? Mohammed is standing here beside you." They will usually say yes. I said to one woman, "I don't know if you're a Muslim, but Mohammed is standing here." She said, "I work in the U.N., and I associate with many Muslims."

I have emphasized that the gifts of the spirit are second to the pursuit of the love of God. There are many gifts of spirit, but the most important one is the gift of being able to love correctly. Various gifts of the spirit allow you to see, hear, touch, taste, smell, and feel the spiritual world. In the New Testament of the Bible, St. Paul describes spiritual gifts as wisdom, knowledge, healing, and the ability to speak in tongues or prophecy, but he clearly states that the greatest gift is love. Each gift is great only when used in service to others, in the context of love.

I rank the spiritual gift of healing higher than clairvoyance, clairaudience, and all spiritual gifts except love, because to use healing as a gift, you must share it with others. Yes, you can heal yourself, but that also requires reaching out to God and those in spirit. It takes a tremendous amount of humility to be used for the healing of yourself or others—to be an instrument or a channel for such loving energy. Healing is one of the greatest ways to express love, whether it's through the laying on of hands, or praying for people who are at a distance. The gift of being able to heal people is the greatest gift except for love, and the two gifts are truly entwined. Love has the power to heal, and healing includes the flow of energy made possible only by loving others as much or more than self.

A spiritually elevated person may exemplify all of the gifts of spirit. When Jesus read the mind of the woman at the well, he was using clairvoyance or clairsentience. Of course, he healed people too. Jesus demonstrated clairvoyance and clairaudience when he spoke with Moses and Elijah, just prior to his crucifixion, and his disciples were using clairvoyance when they perceived this conversation. Jesus had the full spectrum of spiritual gifts, but that was not what motivated him. These gifts came to him as the result of the way he lived, and the result of his sacrificial love for God and humanity. People who are totally dedicated and completely centered on God are those who manifest spirituality at its highest level. Some people call Jesus a great medium. I call him the great physician and great lover of humankind. His love made him capable of doing everything he did.

God and Spiritual Law

Where is God? Jesus said that if a man saw him, he had seen the Father, and St. Paul said that we are temples of God. These statements indicate that the nature and the spirit of God animate us as they animated Jesus. If God ceased to exist, you and I would also cease to exist. Our existence is possible only because of God's eternal quality, his spiritual energy, and his love. We have our lives in him, and he expresses his life through us. The far eastern mystics have repeatedly said that if you want to find God, don't search out among the stars. Go deep inside yourself. Go into the silence, the profound silence. There you'll hear his voice.

I'm sure that many of you hear God's voice within your minds. Because my spiritual senses are easily available to me, I've often heard his voice speaking to me within my mind and even from outside of me. God will often speak to you through the vibration of your own voice. Have you sometimes talked to yourself, in your own mind, to encourage yourself? It's true that some of that is in your thoughts, but much of it is spirit or God speaking to you, through you. If God or spirit spoke to you in unfamiliar voices, you might be startled, so they are careful to use your own vibration, voice, vernacular, and thought channels, at least until you have enough exposure and understanding to be ready to experience the spirit world directly.

Human beings are at the center of the spiritual and physical worlds, and we are intended to have loving and wise dominion over the physical world. We are to take a caring approach to the earth and all of its inhabitants, tending the earth as if it were a garden. But we haven't been wise stewards, and the earth has suffered as a result. It's up to us to straighten out the mess we've made. God isn't going to reach down in some sudden miraculous way and change the human condition or the health of the planet. He will work through enlightened people who can be intellectually and spiritually elevated leaders.

In the vast world of spirit, a hierarchy of love descends from God. Buddha, Mohammed, Lao Tzu, Zoroaster, Moses, and other leaders who founded major religions have had a great positive influence on the way people live morally. In this hierarchy, many great spiritual leaders as well as unsung heroes of the spirit dwell near its apex. They all represent varying degrees of love and truth. Of all founders of religions, Jesus taught the highest *concept*. He taught the truth of truths—that God is the Father of humankind, and we are the sons and daughters of God. Above all, he taught and exemplified the principles of love and forgiveness. This is what makes his teaching the highest in the spiritual world. Great masters in the spirit world have spoken through those on earth to say, "Yes, Jesus' teaching is the highest in the spiritual world." Love is the reason. This does not put those who follow him on the same level spiritually, for unless we live as Jesus lived, we cannot be elevated in love and understanding as he was elevated. It is in *living* out of love and truth that their rewards are manifested in our soul and in our outer circumstances. That is true both on earth and in the spirit world.

I must add that all of the world's religions have been important in leading people up the spiritual ladder to their creator. Granted, different approaches have been taught and advocated, but in the end, due to God's working behind all of these efforts, all will end up in the same place. After all, God is the creator and parent of all, and if he can't find a way to bring everyone home, then we must give up all hope of a sublime, eternal, spiritual life. Life's nature is to lead us ever higher over time, and this tells us that not only is there hope for all to reach the spiritual apex of the spirit world, but that it is also the dream and plan of God. In the end this will be accomplished through the religion of *love!*

The spirit beings who surround us to lead, guide, and encourage us are further along the path than we are, and they are connected to the hierarchy of love at a point reflecting their level of spiritual growth. In turn, they have their own guides and teachers who are above them in the hierarchy, and still others are connected to the hierarchy at a point above them. This chain of love continues until the apex of the hierarchy is reached. There is no arbitrary or punitive reason for where we are in God's hierarchy of love. It all happens according to objective spiritual law, and that law is based entirely on love. We are where we are because of the choices we have made, and we have created our place to be. We would not feel comfortable in the spirit world unless we were in a place where the frequency or energy was not an exact match for our own.

Wherever we are in the hierarchy of love and truth, Jesus and other high guides and teachers can immediately come to us if we sincerely pray for this; but, on a practical level, others routinely work with us on behalf of God or higher spiritual teachers. As we respond to the guidance of those higher in love than we are, and as we reach out to serve those who need our help, we grow, and our place in the hierarchy evolves and changes.

There are schools and universities in the spirit world, and the topic most frequently studied is spiritual law. Beings in the spirit world come to understand spiritual law better than most of us on earth, and they know that energy for spiritual growth exists in the physical body. Our own spirit grows most readily through its interaction with our physical body while we are alive on earth. The physical body is to the human spirit what soil is to a plant. The soil provides the plant with nutrients for growth. For example, a pear tree gets nutrients from the earth, the sunshine and the air. It comes to maturity and bears fruit. The fruit ripens until it's ready to fall off the tree, and we eat it.

According to spiritual law, the spirit and the body have a symbiotic relationship. Spirit grows in conjunction with the physical body as energy is exchanged between the two. The energy that the physical body gives to the spirit enables it to grow to spiritual maturity, and the energy that the spirit gives to the physical body animates it. The physical body dies when the spirit leaves it. When we enter the spirit world, the state of our spirits reflects the thoughts, feelings, and behaviors we experienced during our physical lives on earth. While we live on earth, it is possible to pretend we are something other than we are, and there is sometimes a discrepancy between our inner state and our outer words, appearance, and even behaviors. In the spirit world, our inner nature is completely visible. It is impossible for us to appear or act in ways that do not reflect exactly who we are.

People who live for themselves or commit hurtful acts such as robbery, murder, rape, misuse of the body, or misuse of other people, generate negative energy from their physical bodies that causes their spirits to become stunted or even misshapen. Good works create the best kind of energy for our spiritual growth. There is a strong correlation between the working out of one's inner life and spiritual growth, and the encumbrances of the body. If we didn't have this physical body to contend with, we wouldn't learn as much. For example, those of us who are over fifty years old feel that our minds are young, but our physical bodies don't stay on the same level. As we have more physical challenges and our bodies slow down, we face that reality and learn to become more patient.

What can we do if we enter the spirit world still in need of physical energy to grow spiritually? Most who enter the spirit world do want to further their growth, regardless of how they have lived their earthly lives. To do this, they work with someone on the earth with whom they find rapport. As they help someone else to grow, they receive some of the positive energy generated by that person's physical body, and they also grow. You have heard people say that they learn by teaching. It's much the same principle.

Why Doesn't Everyone Know About the Spirit World?

Many people have seen or received signs from guides, relatives, angels, and other beings. Everyone has at least heard about such experiences. Then why isn't the spirit world accepted universally in the same way that we accept that the sky is blue? One of the reasons, especially in the western world, is that spiritual or mystical experience happens in a dimension that we can't perceive with our physical senses. It is difficult to replicate in a scientific laboratory. Science is moving closer to being able to detect other dimensions, but without hard evidence, a scientist is unlikely to go out on a limb with a theory that is likely to be rejected or ridiculed.

Throughout history, religious and spiritual teachings around the world have recognized the spirit world as reality, though it has been called different things. Buddhists call it Nirvana, where individuality ceases to exist as one merges back into the spirit of God. Hindus believe that we move in and out of the spirit world through many incarnations until a person fulfills the law of karma and is free to exist in a state of heavenly bliss. American Indians have traditionally called the spirit world the Happy Hunting Ground, where food and peace are bountiful. Christians have a variety of concepts: Some sing hymns about Beulah Land, a place where everyone has enough, and lives in joy. Others describe heaven as a place where they will sit with Jesus at a banquet table, meet him on the throne, or experience a peaceful state with God. Some believe their bodies will be glorified and raised up to heaven or that heaven will come on earth, and Jesus will dwell among them. For Jews, the Messiah is yet to come to lead humankind into a better existence.

Many contemporary spiritual leaders who refer to God as *The Source*, *All That Is*, a *Higher Power*, or *Universal Consciousness*, also affirm the existence of angels, spiritual teachers, and spiritual masters who come close to us to encourage and guide us on our journey through life. Those who search for answers on their own may decide that the existence of a creator makes sense when they look at creation. Since they see God as eternal, they conclude that we must be too. People may seek God through reading spiritual books, attending discussion groups, participating in non-dogmatic religious organizations, or engaging in private prayer, meditation, and other spiritual practices. Some search for truth through more than one avenue.

Followers of organized religion may feel that they have all the truth they need through the authority of established teachings and the guidance of earthly spiritual leaders. Those who search for God in less conventional ways must judge for themselves the truth that resonates deep within their souls. Whether we follow a traditional religious teaching or we seek on our own, how do we recognize truth?

The best way to judge any teaching or spiritual experience is to go inside through prayer and meditation to inquire within yourself as to its authenticity. Journaling is a good way to find out more. Simply sit quietly and let your writing flow, perhaps in response to a question you have posed. Before acting on a spiritual inspiration, use your own discernment and speak with someone you trust who can give you a reality check. One good rule of thumb is this: Ask yourself if this information or experience helps you in your daily life. Is it consistent with what you already know in your heart to be true? Does it have a positive impact on you and those around you?

Because God is spirit, we can't see him with the physical senses, but we do experience God by going inside and knowing him through our hearts, our emotions. Sometimes in settings where we're moved by beautiful, uplifting music, tears come to our eyes, and we feel chills or a rush of warmth. This is a spiritual reality, not a physical reality, and it happens often. When I was growing up, one of the reasons I looked forward to going to church was to feel this beautiful energy.

When you speak of loved ones who have already passed into the spirit world or have moving thoughts of them, have you ever felt a sudden warmth, a tingling, or goose bumps? Each of us generates and is surrounded by our own spiritual energy field called an aura, and when spirit moves close to us, their energy touches ours, and we feel the effects. We know instinctively whether the energy coming near us is high or low, positive or negative. The same thing is true when we are near positive or negative energy on earth. These experiences happen to many of us, but unless we understand them, we may miss the signals.

There are people from all religious backgrounds who know that spirit world exists through undeniable first-hand experiences. They have visitations from relatives who are living in the spiritual world, and this happens in dreams, at their bedsides, or while they are going about their daily tasks. The fact is that the spiritual world is even more real than the physical world. The physical earth, in all of its beauty, is only a pale reflection of the spiritual world.

What do you do if you are skeptical about the idea of God and the spirit world? If you are in this category, my advice is to be alert to the possibility of life after death, and listen for your own inner guidance about the information you receive and the experiences you have. At the very least, once you have the perspective given here, you will be better prepared should you find yourself still conscious after your own physical death.

I've never met a human being who didn't have curiosity to some degree. The desire to know drives us on to acquire still more knowledge. When you stop learning, you stop growing. Many people who have had near-death experiences report that two questions are usually asked of them: "Did you learn?" and "Did you love?" That is what life is all about. If you are not learning, and you're not growing in love, then you are missing something in your spiritual life.

Pursue truth with your whole life, to the very end, until you know experientially whether there is or isn't a spirit world. I left no stone unturned in pursuit of this question, and I think that's why God has honored me with the experiences I have been given. I now feel that my greatest responsibility in this life is to share these very real experiences.

I do not suggest everyone should become a professional medium. In fact, I recommend against it, unless you feel a persistent calling to this profession, because you must sacrifice a great deal, and your life is not your own. I do recommend that you pursue the truth of life, the truth of things, with everything you have. Your answers may not come in the way that mine did, but they will come according to who you are and what your need is. *However* they come, if you are sincere, they will come from one source, the Creator of all, our Father in heaven who actively lives and has his being in you. That I know.

In that place where love reigns supreme, all that you have ever desired that is good and loving will be yours, and the presence of divine love will be palpable and all-pervasive. From this is derived eternal peace and joy in a world populated by those who have mastered life by mastering love.

Mastery Press

Phoenix, Arizona

For general inquiries send an email to
PB@PhilipBurley.com, or write to:

Adventures in Mastery, LLC (AIM)
P.O. Box 43548
Phoenix, AZ 85080

For more information about Philip Burley
and the work of
Adventures in Mastery, LLC,
please visit this website:
www.PhilipBurley.com